Something in writing

David Broadbridge

Oversteps Books

First published in 2017 by   Oversteps Books Ltd
                                          6 Halwell House
                                          South Pool
                                          Nr Kingsbridge
                                          Devon
                                          TQ7 2RX
                                          UK

www.overstepsbooks.com

Copyright © 2017 David Broadbridge
ISBN 978-1-906856-69-4

All rights reserved. No part of this book may be reproduced, stored in a retrieval system, or transmitted in any form, or by any means, electronic, mechanical, photocopying, recording or otherwise, or translated into any language, without prior written permission from Oversteps Books, except by a reviewer who may quote brief passages in a review.

The right of David Broadbridge to be identified as the author of this work has been asserted by him in accordance with the Copyright, Designs and Patents Act 1988.

Printed in Great Britain by imprint digital, Devon

for Deborah

Notes and Acknowledgements

Acknowledgements are due to the editors of the following where some of these poems appeared for the first time: *Acumen, Equinox, The French Literary Review, The Frogmore Papers, The Liberal, The Oxford Magazine, The Oxford Theologian, Resurgence and Ecologist, The SHOp, Templar Poetry, The Warwick Review.*

The Southwold Sailors' Reading Room won third prize in the 'Writing at Sea' competition, 2014.
The Republic of Glassblowing was originally commissioned to celebrate the 90th birthday of Helen Suzman.
Great House takes its inspiration from Joan Barton's *Great House on View Day.*
The quotations in *For Bix Beiderbecke* are taken from 'A New History of Jazz' by Alyn Shipton and from a book review by Philip Larkin.
A shortened version of *O Magnum Mysterium* has been set to music as a carol by Christopher Gower and is available from Encore Publications.

Also by David Broadbridge: *Treading the Dance* - Danish Mediaeval Ballads (translation).

Contents

Something in writing	1
The republic of glassblowing	2
The early light	4
The juggler	5
Gap year	6
Edward Thomas's watch	8
Migration	9
John Clare: Northampton asylum, 1852	10
Snow days	11
The uses of the globe	12
The quilt	14
A peach of a day	15
The old house	16
The waistcoat	17
For Bix Beiderbecke	18
A picture of geese	19
Her afterlife	20
The red balloon	21
Great house	22
Burial party	24
Particularly Kent	25
The white rose	26
Street evangelist	27
Wash day	28
Kynance Cove	29
In a second-hand bookshop	30
Flight path	31
Rembrandt: the suicide of Lucretia	32
To see it all again	33
The railway children	34
Magellan's boyhood at Sabrosa	35
Mappa mundi	36
Daylight saving time	38
Derailed	39
The Southwold Sailors' Reading Room	40

My father conducts Beethoven	42
Suffragette	43
Cheiranthus	44
O magnum mysterium	45
The marsh country	46

Something in writing

They were always a lesson, those anonymous scribes,
who hour by assiduous hour gifted us the carried weight
of each gospel page, the colour-heavy capitals,

their Alphas and Omegas, enamelled and ornate:
a testament blown from a Horn of Plenty
or carried on a dolphin's cursive back,

migrating across borders, feather-light:
an uplift, like the smallest bird from any branch,
writing for the Word's abidance not their name.

And so I would become myself, inclined like them
to work the pages into life, *discipulus,* disciple,
disciplined into flight.

The republic of glassblowing

I.

The glassblower has drawn a crowd.
Like tricoteuses we sit and watch,
as the gob of glass gathers on the marble.
How fragile it seems, this hot nurturing
into the shape he knows we cannot see.
Glass, he tells us, until it becomes
permanent, is as hot and malleable
as a rallied crowd, molten at its edges,
until the centre cools; its laws
and boundaries so easily broken.

II.

How fragile are our institutions, how slow
their flowing into life; the routes they take
across a continent of longing: their long
drawn out arrival: their erratic advocates;
the serious and insubstantial men:
survival of the richest, the shallow graves,
the poor without their walls, the death of kings.
How slow the infancy of making.
Sometimes, we wonder if imagination
must accommodate the rest.

III.

We watch and wait and hold our breath,
at this pausable moment,
the make or break of working
something into shape: he knows the risks,
is lost in concentration; his breath
becomes as fluent as the changeful glass.
And what he gives us, as he crafts
it into life, is the benevolent
breathing of a liberal voice,
to make a bright constituency:
a transparent jubilation, through which
we see the shape we want our lives to be;
the long, slow, rising republican note,
unbroken, as it cools and toughens into fixity.

The early light

The early light today is Turner's light
across the open landscape of the plain.

An old way, like a parting,
tapers to Blake's clouded hills,

above, a jet is riding westwards,
chalking its trail across the sky.

Here is a history made sayable
of England's old domains,

of gods consoling, unconsoled:
like broken tesserae on a mosaic floor,

a Viking keel quenching in the sand,
a shower of arrows shot at Agincourt,

oaks felled for an Armada,
the cry of martyrs taken to the fire,

England's inner echoing,
like something hidden until heard,

as sounds are in the tongues of bells,
so that here, despite the air's erosion

on each face, you feel earthed and steadied
between the backwards and forwards of time,

while high above the jet trail has now hazed,
and leaves the stones and us still standing.
                              Both amazed.

The juggler

An evening sunshaft in the city square
has picked the juggler out. In the illustrated
shadows, a concentrated crowd is enthralled

as he makes five coloured balls sing against
the sky; timed parabolas, a moving arch,
in the sweet curve of their space-time laws.

We're almost willing one to fall,
but he lets us down. Instead, we catch
our breath as the rhythm of his hand and eye

begins to mesmerise. And as we watch,
it seems he has set in motion something else.
The same laws that keep each ball in play

maintain the equilibrium of stars,
the pull of moon-worked tides.
These unresting stations of the air,

draw us on beyond an apple's fall
to foundations older and more near-fetched
than the ordered balance of our lives.

But as the shadows and the crowd disperse,
the lovers who take each other's hands
are closer to him than anything I know.

His language of the hand and eye provides,
they seem to say, in its audaciousness,
an unexpected entrance to the heart,

as if to prove hand to hand, and eye to eye,
the speechless co-ordinates of love's art.

Gap year

The Paris crowds are arriving,
trailing their black lozenge cases,
their frequent-traveller faces
tired with the details of late-night deals.

Behind the barrier we're waiting
to get you in our sights again,
to see your lopsided grin,
vying to be the first to say,
after a year away, 'There he is.'
The big shock is your head is shaved,
skull-blue: Belsen-headed by choice.

The platform dissolves into a swarm
of khaki bodies, brylcreamed partings,
blanco, webbing, kitbags,
voices on the edge of laughter,
and me thinking they must have been
about your age ...
                    ... thinking of one war,
and then another, your great-grandfather
asleep in the square at Rouen,
his postcard on the kitchen table...
                                ... coming back
through Picardy, courtesy of Eurostar,
those were his fields you were going past;
his six-month, deadly, slow advance,
within a quick minute ...

In sleep you seem to wear my father's face,
and his face dissolves into another's again.
He must have been about your age.
Demobbed, he would have given
that same grin, back from it all, at last,
miraculously unmarked,
but by everything he'd seen and done,
forever changed within.

Next morning, your mother, love itself,
woke you late with tea, after a night
when you might have been
dead to the world.

Edward Thomas's watch

stopped at 7.36 a.m.
Easter Monday 9th April 1917.
And suddenly coming into focus is
England: the softly dipping meadows,
that moment when *the noonday heat
defrauds the lilies of their dew,*
old grey hop poles,
the serenity of poppies,
a lane of larches that he loved:
all suddenly stopped in time.

Migration

The birds are flying south.
As regular as the tide or visiting moon
their time has come again.

All day they have been gathering,
threading themselves into the moment
never quite touching, yet so in touch

the spaces between them almost obliterate.
They trust each instinct, each membrane,
as their clatter disarranges the sky.

Expected elsewhere, they are suddenly gone,
have become historic, leaving behind
the high September, emptied air.

Their going attunes me to the season:
the thump of falling apples,
first mist in the hard stubble,

leaving, as they arrived, out of the blue.

John Clare: Northampton asylum, 1852

Another visitor finds him at work in the kitchen-garden behind one of the wings of the asylum. They fall into conversation, walk around the grounds and then go into Clare's room. It was an apartment pleasantly situated, having a garden beneath the windows. There was a birdcage, with a skylark in it, near the window, and pointing to the iron bars in his apartment, he smiled gloomily and said in a strong provincial accent, "We are both of us bound birds, you see."

John Clare, *Jonathan Bate*

'Watching the morning hatch to light,
sets me thinking of a clear spring river
coursing like quicksilver
round the curve of the ditch,

and the rainbow and brown trout
jumping out of themselves
as if they wanted more freedom
than the river can give,

and the trees everywhere I look
coming into green,
and a light shower
coaxing the grain,

and me having my natural freedom
like the badger, pheasant and fox,
and infinite April here,
and the Winter behind,

and me thinking of roads
that travel has to find.'

Snow days

September to July, I taught
them all the power of words,

but every year I lost my sway
when snow began to faintly fall.

As winter showcased itself
against the glass, they turned

excited from each page as each tiny flake
airbrushed my words away.

Snow outlives us, real snow I mean,
as words do, too; they have their time.

Knowing this, you find that reading on,
can once more make them faintly fall,

imagination gifting us a world,
white silence filling up the room again.

The uses of the globe

'Men have forgotten this truth,' said the fox,
'but you must not forget it. You become
responsible for ever for what you have tamed.'
　　　　　　　　The Little Prince, *Antoine de Saint Exupery*

That picture of the earth, you know, the one
they took from Apollo 8, shows us so beautiful
against the dark immensities of space,
the oceans and the land about as big
as the little lighted globe that you once had
beside your bed, and could set in motion
with your powerful Sistine fingertip.

Remember, too, when you were young,
writing your name inside your books,
the whole address traversed the page:
street and town, then country and continent –
a separate line allowed for each –
until you placed yourself within *The World*
and with a final boast, *The Universe*.

You could now touch the Earth to life
on any screen held in your hand,
then cut it down to size by zooming in
to find the street where once you lived.
But the oceans and the land today
are nothing like that globe you spun,
and we have turned so many times in sleep

since then, to wake and find the weather
disturbs us now; the rising waters break
upon our shores; the Arctic ice drip feeds
into the sea, the heat that left the sun today
has burned the backs on every beach.
We thought that we were hosts to plenitude,
instead we find that we are paying guests.

And we are not the first or final selves
to wonder at the staggering Earth.
Our little globe, lit from within,
should still require from us
(for what it's worth) the custody of joy,
serve to remind us of our numbered hairs,
the moment of a sparrow's fall.

It's taken us till now to reassure
ourselves of what we doubt, but since there is
no greater wealth than life itself,
working as one heart to gather in
our scattered strength might prove to be
our consolation prize, and be enough to know
that just, by being human, we survive?

The quilt

All year the wedding quilt spread on the frame,
the flowering pattern of its brilliant
mauves and greens displayed your gift each day,
as the tiny rice grains of each stitch
furrowed their way across the counterpane.

Some months I could not call to see
the steady progress that you made,
but when I did the wonder was at any
long-laboured, handmade thing.

Towards the end you called me up
to watch you sew the fault-line in.
You wanted me to understand
how it would be 'a prideful thing'
to think that we can make perfection
in our lives when only God is so.

But for days now, the sense that something else
was being woven in has filled my thoughts:
that you were harvesting a loss
of something you had sowed,
something set aside or under-lived,
and were unable to retrieve it
from lying fallow from so long ago.

A peach of a day

I

Like plump cardinals in vermillion conclave,
a dozen stately peaches sit on purple tissue
in a small white-latticed wooden tray,
as my father walks towards me
in southern sunlight. One, an even
darker red towards its sun-struck stalk,
was what my hovering hand thought best
to choose; its first touch and taste
as vivid and familiar to that boy today.

II

Peaches then were only summer fruit,
but now they can be bought *ad lib*,
I find my father is in season all the year;
and since resemblance, not unlikeness
is the source for variations of the same,
to bite on one on any day,
of any week, of any month, of any year,
brings back once more his durable trace
each time the juice runs down my chin again.

The old house

We had lived in the old house long enough
to know its every mood and shift:
the wind that rattled in the sash,
the split logs settling in the grate,
the give of floorboards as we climbed to sleep,
the steep stairs rising with the latch.

Unroofed, the quadrants of each room by night
would show another view: two lying close
and two asleep, one fast beside a lamp
in case she woke, one turning to
the summons of his dream. It was
our breathing and their rising space.

Their flat-packed drawings of the house
were nothing like the house itself,
except for one instinctive touch
that memory has not mislaid.
There was no straight path to the door,
bright flowers sprawling either side,

no childish four-squared window frames
at which neat curtain-curves were drawn,
but rising from the steep-pitched roof
their artless hands would always colour in
remembered warmth: that curl of smoke
the final crayoned master-stroke.

The waistcoat

Eddie Doherty made the waistcoat
I am wearing as I write this poem,
at the loom behind his shop
in Ardara, County Donegal,

where you can watch, he says
the tweed come to life,
where the warp and weft of it
takes days to thread, like verse.

The day I bought it I felt
woven into words again:
'Health to wear,' he said,
his handshake both a blessing and farewell.

For Bix Beiderbecke

What they remembered was what they said:

Midwest campus venues,
Bix and the gang, tuxedoed
behind the monogrammed music desks,

and the past midnight slow tempos,
when the dancers' bodies are 'glued
so close together as if they tried
to move through each other'.

Self-taught, pitch perfect, save what
he learned from passing riverboats,
'his best trick was to name each note
in any ten-fingered chord you'd care to strike';

his long flighted solos were 'like shooting
bullets at a bell,' or 'that moment when a girl says yes.'
Genius cannot be helped: aged twenty-eight,
'that nice boy' drank himself to death.

A picture of geese
for Else Pia Martinsen Erz

Each time you try to capture them
you know you'll not succeed.
Though all the birds within you rise
and each canvas becomes the net
to catch them on, they always stream away,
like daylight lessening in the west.

Though that's the insufficiency of art
yet how it suffices: wings and hands
outstretched, plying the sky's wet canvas,
both in your element, your brain and theirs
fixing the tilt of each wing
in flight: perfect, near perfect.

Her afterlife
When you hear of his death, tell me immediately. I am not a fool.
                                                    Fanny Brawne

She has been walking the Heath,
or has taken to her room
to read his letters
over and again,
as if for the first time.
Her hair is cut widow-short.

She wears black.
Her life has widened inwards
to learn that losing love
is differently sad
from any other loss
she has to bear.

The night before,
she walks the Heath again.
The darkness waits
to deepen into day,
and high above
the strange dark acres

give a sweet unrest.
The moon comes up and stays,
and one bright star
has ventured out,
as if to prove itself,
Keatsian in its steadfastness.

It takes three weeks
for the news to reach her
from Rome.
That morning
when she wakes
she has already heard it.

The red balloon

One summer morning, hours before dawn,
I lay awake, imagining in a lush field

a tethered red balloon before it lifted off,
released to rise against the air's soft yield.

Last night, in late August light, brought
it all to life again. Above the house,

one silently appeared. We watched,
until a sudden pulse of flame

maintained and then increased its height
and took it out of view.

I turned and saw with that same burn
that first lit our days, your anchored eyes

catch mine, fastened still and still surprised
by our ebullient flight.

Great house

The long straight drive through avenues of trees,
where fallow-deer drift in and out of view,
leads down towards a lake with swans at ease,
past lawns edged round with sentinels of yew,
until, beyond the gatehouse and parterre,
the serious façade at last appears,
shouldering off the wide-surrounding air.

From the pillared entrance hall, a staircase
rises in two shallow flights to the Great Hall
where, above the enormous fireplace,
self-centred portraits overwhelm the wall,
all looking down as if they claimed some prize,
though at face value, and this close distance,
there's scarcely anyone we recognise.

Some rooms have shutters that are closed to keep
the sunlight from the fading silk: no books
are read, the fruit is wax, the carved and deep
upholstered chairs have little ropes on hooks,
and further on the dining room is laid
for some house-party guests who never come;
it all feels like a curious masquerade.

Past tapestries and Chinese lacquered screens,
small suits of armour and rich inlaid chests
past porcelain and fragile figurines,
more paintings of men grandly overdressed,
each swagged and gilded space gives out a sense,
as room after room recedes from view,
of an abundant emptiness.

Someone real should still be living here,
looking out across this landscaped air,
someone, perhaps, polishing their verses,
knowing they have a reason to be there,
while in the copse beyond, teeming life abounds,
and down long-shadowed avenues of trees,
virgins walk with unicorns in the laurelled grounds.

Burial party

Late summer heat, the sunflash on the screen
meant I almost missed the sign, whose message
jauntily askew, directed family and friends to
'Dad's Death Do.'

A flock of bright balloons led down
a tree-lined drive, past candles wax-wavering
in tiny jars, to a black-timbered barn.

A band was playing ragtime. Each wistful
and heart-stirring tune seemed scored
to make the mourners feel almost immune
to what they'd come to mark.

I thought no more about it until next day
I saw the scene replay itself, and felt
this is how we balance loss these days:

unsure of Heaven, no longer scared of Hell,
our pain subsumed in celebration
and quickening laughter in the air again.

Particularly Kent

Right on cue the blossom arrives,
transforms the trees, transforms our lives,
its sudden swathes of colour bring
a sense of summer into spring.

It only seems to last a week,
its seven day show a winning streak
we know must end: and then it's past
like sunlight off reflecting glass.

Because we know how brief is bliss,
we should live our days like this,
catch each blown petal as it falls,
revel in their bright applause.

The white rose
i.m. Sophie Scholl 1921-1943

What you can hear from above,
Sophie, is the sound my pen is making
as it unearths you; you and your wilful

candidacy for grace, your ungovernable
regard for truth as you looked up and ahead.
'Someone had to make a start,' you said,

as the ungrieving ground thawed by degrees
in late February sun sublime.
You knew all along to what it led.

The distance that you travelled
just to cross that room I could never do,
but that is why your uncalendared days

have been sent on ahead of you,
to await our late arrival.
So what you can hear is the sound

my pen is making, preparing the ground
for you, *un beau geste*, spreading out
the root ball of a white rose,

in late February sun sublime:
making sure in a growing season,
that now you are well planted.

Street evangelist

Pitch perfect, black book in hand,
his voice, thick with imperatives,
swirls through the crowd,
then narrows, like a hardening vein,
to tell me that I am a sinful man,
more stripped of glory than arrayed,
and all around me are alike consigned.

His high-wire act is taut with choice,
his hands beseech, then gesture wide
as if to fix himself; there is no doubt,
from where he stands, between damnation
and the everlasting arms.

He seems as much like all those others
as he is himself : those drawn
to standing stones, or statues
weeping blood, the chosen ones,
envisioning, hands held aloft ,
wild-eyed, forever looking out
for the kingdom that lies within.

Wash day

There was the wash tub with a dough of sheets
wrung out through rollers, the wooden clothes horse,
its canvas hinges seeping specks of rust,

and I would come home to windows steamed
with the opaque fuzz of my mother's work
condensed to dry; the beads of silver danced

on the iron's triangle as she clumped the board.
I would watch her plane a sheet, tuck each corner
neat-wise into its white oblong, until

everything was smoothed, then I would
bear it up, a trophy for a king, and watch
amazed as we laid out its warm purity:

and there each time her love for him
was spread out clear to see, embedded
like the diamond fold in the centre of the sheet.

Kynance Cove

You are forever arriving here,
where marine light over the rises
recolours the gorse,

and salvoes of light flash
off the rain-sheen of slate,
to where the path dips down

its last green turning
to a clutter of rock falls
waves sleek and darken.

Best of all those times,
when, in the slack days
of summer we drive late

through accumulating dark,
stripped of the city lights,
hedges blurring into edges,

down through soft Devon,
until impervious Cornwall
wakes you, having slept.

As slow, morning sunlight
fastens its warmth, here you stand,
confronting the weather, looking out

from yourself, into yourself:
earthed, like the sea, ready
for your face-off with copious life.

In a second-hand bookshop

Inside the flyleaf, something tucked:
not the usual newspaper cutting,
forgotten list or honeymoon pressed flower,

but a small, blue envelope,
(long kept or just mislaid?) the letter
folded and unfolded so many times
that what was once a crease is now a tear.

I think that snow was falling when she left,
(the winter date), but not enough to cover up
this faint acoustic of her steps, nor how,

suddenly, in a second-hand bookshop,
a life laid bare,
touches me with words like this:

'love never fails,' but fails the heart,
what then, for all our love, can love repair?

Flight path

Tivoli Gardens carousel, and for
Alfred, aged two, this is the ride
he has been waiting for all his life.

His mother behind him is holding him
as tight as he holds the reins of his chosen horse.
A lifetime's wait it seems until the music starts

and the carousel begins its slow revolve.
Each time he passes we exchange a wave.
He's spinning faster now and faster still,

the flying horses taut on their hawsers
flung out towards us like his grin.
What now, I wonder, if his horse

breaks free and suddenly propels him
high into the Copenhagen sky
on a magic horse amongst the stars,

like in his storybooks, riding with ease,
never looking back, telling his mother
not to fear, telling her this is my future now,

that the day will come when she must
let go, though all she'll want to do
is hold on for dear life.

Rembrandt: the suicide of Lucretia

Dying in a painting ought to be easier than this;
think of how they do it in opera or ballet,
the beauty of the dying swan,
Mimi or Violetta singing their hearts out
in a final glorious aria of melodious song,

and then the curtain call, the bravoed applause,
flowers strew the stage, the diva finally appears
her hand across her heart, left and right,
up to the Gods she acknowledges the crowd
then slowly stoops into her long final bow.

But nothing like that is happening here:
death and the dagger have drawn you on
as the moon draws water, and this seeping stain
across the wounded moon of your breast
makes me imagine the next freeze frame,

your legs will have given way,
that rope you are holding will have tightened,
and your death will bring a different house down;
and across this most terrible dissolution,
your eyes seem to be achieving a bridge with me.

So, you must imagine me writing this years hence,
somewhere under a lamp, full of the knowledge
of what you lost and won; thinking how strong and sad
you are, like a wounded bird settling at evening,
straightening a wing that has folded wrong.

To see it all again

Late December, and at morning, I still felt
some warmth on my clouded window
when I found the queen bee lying drowsed.

Throughout the day I checked her movement,
but she stayed, her instincts weather-tuned
for when she had to make her move.

I warmed to her as down-payment
on the year ahead, her settlement
a reflected need, a stored reward to claim

if she should see this winter out,
when in the swarming cloister of the hive
she could renew her reign,

and another morning when a rim
of light would waken us to blossom
on the trees, going south.

The railway children

When we stood at the end
of the platform it was always the big names
we wanted to see, so that morning

when *Mallard* backed on we knew
our luck was in: we watched
the gentle push and give of coupled coaches,

marked in our book this famous name.
Invited up, we felt the slab of heat
as tendered coal turned white-hot in the fire-box.

You sat in the driver's cracked-leather
bucket seat from where you blew the whistle
and suddenly unroofed a flight of birds,

from their high-girdered perch.
Back down to earth, and scaled so small
beside the massive red-rimmed wheels,

we waited for the signal's nod:
a wave was given and returned,
oiled pistons thrust and swathed

in steam she slowly left behind
her outlined length of streamlined air.
Remember how we were together then,

my dear brother? Stand beside me here again.
Feel the heat blast from the fire-box take you back.
Hear that lonesome whistle blow.

Magellan's boyhood at Sabrosa

That morning he must have raised his eyes
in the sun-struck, heat-slabbed square
to a point beyond and smelled there
the salt air where white coasts called,

narrowed his gaze to where
the world rolled over in his mind,
turned it, as he turned in sleep,
into something that could be done.

Like the lizard clamped in frozen grace
upon the tavern wall, he must have
centred it in his mind
so it became a fixture, a fixation,

until the moment came when the long road
out of Sabrosa took him out of sight
and into the world's fame, measuring his strides
by the slow rotations of the globe.

Mappa mundi

*Now would I give a thousand furlongs of sea for an acre
of barren ground: long heath, broom, furze, anything.*
                    Shakespeare: The Tempest, Act I Scene 1

Those sea-discoverers that to new worlds
had gone, who laid out their flat maps
to conceive a globe, narrowed their gaze
to a fixation, then found under
their spread fingertips they were scaled
not to find a route, but shape a space.

The maps they knew compelled them out
from shuttered rooms in heat-struck squares,
out beyond the crowded harbour walls,
the cannons' timed salute, conscripted them
to bring the far-fetched close to hand.

O to be the first to reach new lands,
after compassed nights with firmaments of stars
and days of wearied sameness on the sea,
to feel soaked timbers ease and quench
in sand, slide into shallows, feel firmness
at your feet then wade waist deep to shore,

taste cinnamon and cloves, pour out cascades
of stones, sail on the tide to realms of gold:
to place on every tongue the name America,
the Indies, the Azores, the waters
of your wake forever traced and clarified.

But circumference means coming back
to realise the perfect cadences that sent them out
– *Endeavour, Resolution, Enterprise* –
those names they gave each laden caravel,
resolve themselves to their home key,

relearning how, to their surprise,
the local cuts far deeper than the world
and takes us into consecrated ground,
far-fetched discoverers again, sated with distance,
the earth once more at our fingertips,
dividing our time between this world and the next.

Daylight saving time
for Emma

For some time now, I have been trying
to work out what holds you together.

I could run through a thesaurus
to find synonyms for courage,

but that's a commonplace with you,
and bravery's about the same.

It may be some of those, but if hearing
is the last sense that they say we lose,

it might instead be what I heard this morning,
when I woke early and listened

to a chorus line of birds singing,
just because the day had come to light.

Derailed

My train pulls in alongside another,
voices call, a whistle sounds
and we begin to move, or so I think.

But then, as sometimes happens,
when I look again it is the other
which has moved away.

Suddenly, I feel adrift with that same
stabbing sense when our illusions go
and we have stumbled,

almost unnoticed, into loss, as though
something seeming permanent
like *Love* or *God* simply wasn't so.

The Southwold Sailors' Reading Room

Because all roads in England run finally
to the sea, I have come here through long,
flat Suffolk country miles to where
the sea and sky cohere in Southwold.

To step inside *The Sailors' Reading Room*
is to occupy another time,
where face to face I meet Mick Mayhew,
Slimmy Ashmenall and Jumbo Hurr,
and next to them citations hung
when duty burned its message
on their brain: 'For lives they gallantly saved,'
and 'Their actions were humanity's proof.'

Their pictures show them being praised,
or the moment when the medal is pinned.
Rank-aware, they stand deferential,
in the presence of each eminence:
a bushy Admiral, a paunchy Lord,
even some minor foreign King. One is shy,
another has his gaze quite fixed ahead.

Each seems to say, why am I the focus
of this act and not the man I saved?
What did I do to merit this, when,
at the moon's cold insistence,
the sea heaved its catalogue
of souls and waves into a unity
of fear? From blank side streets
we'd always come at any time:
at blackening dusk, or lightened day
or when a false light has been swung
and wreckers know the best and worst will come.

And these other pictures, too, of casual-seeming
men, playing crib in the *Lord Nelson* snug,
shuffling the pack, joking, waiting contemplating,
fussing over pigeons or plot;
what do they do now, sitting still here
in *The Southwold Sailors' Reading Room*?
What awaits them? Brushy Watson, Frank Upcraft,
Winner Smith, back from that night of all nights
when they got the Dutchman off, but still he died?

What else can they do now, back from the ruthless,
running sea or the beckoning moon,
but learn the truth of every hero's story:
how to live out long ordinary days
after crowded hours of glory.

My father conducts Beethoven

My father in the living room,
has his music turned up loud,
a poker from the hearth in hand,

poised to conduct a score he knows by heart.
The rhythm of his beat
configures the air above my head,

so that even the rests are not a silence,
but another space in which the music moves,
and he steps out of this world

into the *Apotheosis of the Dance*.
I used to think of him at work,
unschooled, obscured and unsought,

but that here at least he had found
another way by which his days were graced.
And now, but backlit by memory,

with all the clarity that distance gives,
another father is lost in the music,
one who never had the furtherance

that choice or chance can bring
and so seemed always incomplete,
as if he knew there was another life

he could conduct, but never did:
the way two lives lie parallel, *ad infinitum,*
but only in the mind's eye ever meet.

Suffragette

You said resistance must be learned,
no borders in your head,
fighting against the practised sameness
of the times: no conformity,
the peaks honed down, the valleys filled.

Next day you were front page,
but the indifferent crowd
cared more about the horse's fall
than your collision course.

What you did reverberates minutely
still, as a seismograph registers
the shock miles below,
the jerked needle suddenly rising,

and when, each time, your fortunate sisters
queue to exercise or spurn
the choice you would never know.

Cheiranthus

Scent from heaven, heaven-scent,
gillyflower, wallflower, planted,
they say, in castle walls
and moated granges
so the heady fragrance would invade
the air and perfume all the rooms.

If this is true, I'd like to think
that on a sun-struck day,
when radiating heat had made
these flowers smell so sweet,
some invader half-way up a castle wall
was so struck by this clove-scentedness,

he toppled backwards from his scaled height,
gave up the day job of laying siege
to the beleagured keep, and falling
slowly to the indenting earth,
knew this was a perfume to die for:
sent to heaven, heaven-scent.

O magnum mysterium

That animals should be the first to see
a baby in their manger laid, would not
to them seem strange.

They would be unsurprised
at what was second nature to their lives,
the laboured birth, the push for life,
the first breath's cry, the skeins
of blood that streaked the straw.

But they were surely taken by surprise
when a lifted latch of widening light
brought star-struck faces in from shires,

or after days of growing quiet had passed
they smelt sweet spices in the raftered air
and met the mild interrogation of distant eyes.

They must have shifted in their stalls,
their breath like gossip rising everywhere,
and thought it odd, not that a baby had been born,
(they'd seen it all before and took him
as they found him, nothing minding)

but that strange kings and shepherds came
who told them of an angel and a star,
and that the child they called the Christ
was worth the finding.

The marsh country

All words of sense, past perfect most,
have made the marsh: moor log,

leaf mould, the peat below,
hair roots of grass go eight feet down,

tap into black underwater ooze
where forest oaks have turned to stone.

Between the inland scarps of cliff
the descent to bleached mounds of shingle,

the fields, proportioned to their need,
answer only to the widespread light,

and never to the question you might ask:
how does such flat land hide itself so well?

Night-haunting smugglers down
the sluiced spaces knew:

knew where to lie in wait, sea-sunk,
for the owl call, before the runs began,

and when the blue lights flashed
a tindered spark would answer.

One night they pegged a Revenue Man
to the shore, and listened to him drown,

then loosened him at dawn next day,
his only trace, the ruffled sand.

Sometimes, as they say, you might think of it
as the *fifth quarter of the globe*,

a floating balance of earth and sky
under cloud-thrown shadows.

Best time is Spring, when the quarter's
green and blue with the loose-leaf feel of life,

and all the rivers of April run again.

Oversteps Books Ltd

The Oversteps list includes books by the following poets:

David Grubb, Giles Goodland, Alex Smith, Will Daunt, Patricia Bishop, Christopher Cook, Jan Farquarson, Charles Hadfield, Mandy Pannett, Doris Hulme, James Cole, Helen Kitson, Bill Headdon, Avril Bruton, Marianne Larsen, Anne Lewis-Smith, Mary Maher, Genista Lewes, Miriam Darlington, Anne Born, Glen Phillips, Rebecca Gethin, W H Petty, Melanie Penycate, Andrew Nightingale, Caroline Carver, John Stuart, Rose Cook, Jenny Hope, Hilary Elfick, Anne Stewart, Oz Hardwick, Terry Gifford, Michael Swan, Maggie Butt, Anthony Watts, Robert Stein, Graham High, Ross Cogan, Ann Kelley, A C Clarke, Diane Tang, R V Bailey, John Daniel, Alwyn Marriage, Kathleen Kummer, Jean Atkin, Charles Bennett, Elisabeth Rowe, Marie Marshall, Ken Head, Robert Cole, Cora Greenhill, John Torrance, Michael Bayley, Christopher North, Simon Richey, Lynn Roberts, Sue Davies, Mark Totterdell, Michael Thomas, Ann Segrave, Helen Overell, Rose Flint, Denise Bennett, James Turner, Sue Boyle, Jane Spiro, Jennie Osborne, John Daniel, Janet Loverseed, Wendy Klein, Sally Festing, Angela Stoner, Simon Williams, Susan Taylor, Richard Skinner, Fokkina McDonnell and Joan McGavin.

For details of all these books, information about Oversteps and up-to-date news, please look at our website and blog:

www.overstepsbooks.com
http://overstepsbooks.wordpress.com